Newbern City Library
220 East Main St.
Newbern, TN 38059
731-627-3153

The Word Wizard's Book of SYNONYMS and ANTONYMS

Robin Johnson

Crabtree
Publishing
Company
www.crabtreebooks.com

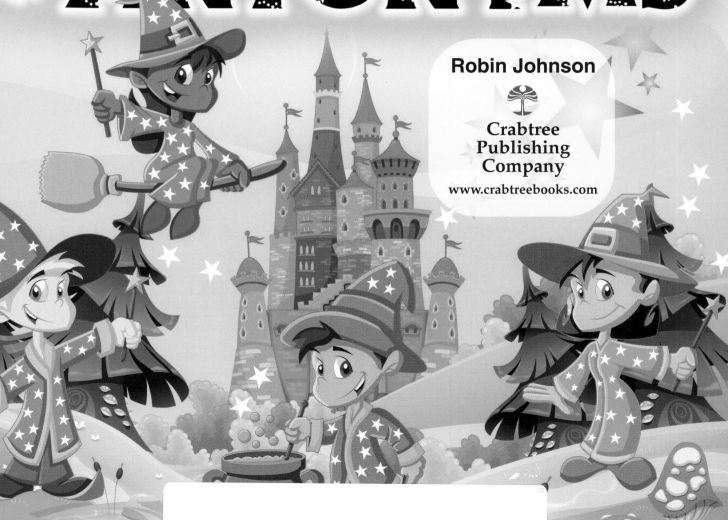

Word Wizard

Author
Robin Johnson

Publishing plan research and development
Reagan Miller

Editorial director
Kathy Middleton

Project coordinator
Kelly Spence

Editor
Anastasia Suen

Proofreader and indexer
Wendy Scavuzzo

Photo research
Robin Johnson, Katherine Berti

Design & prepress
Katherine Berti

Print coordinator
Katherine Berti

Photographs
Dreamstime: p. 10 (left); p. 11 (right)
All other images from Shutterstock

Library and Archives Canada Cataloguing in Publication

Johnson, Robin (Robin R.), author
        The word wizard's book of synonyms and antonyms / Robin
Johnson.

(Word wizard)
Includes index.
Issued in print and electronic formats.
ISBN 978-0-7787-1923-6 (bound).--ISBN 978-0-7787-1927-4 (pbk.).--
ISBN 978-1-4271-7795-7 (pdf).--ISBN 978-1-4271-7791-9 (html)

        1. English language--Synonyms and antonyms--Juvenile literature.
I. Title.

PE1591.J64 2015   j428.1   C2014-907806-4
                                                       C2014-907807-2

Library of Congress Cataloging-in-Publication Data

Johnson, Robin (Robin R.)
 The Word Wizard's book of synonyms and antonyms / Robin Johnson.
     pages cm. -- (Word Wizard)
 Includes index.
 ISBN 978-0-7787-1923-6 (reinforced library binding) --
ISBN 978-0-7787-1927-4 (pbk.) -- ISBN 978-1-4271-7795-7 (electronic pdf) --
ISBN 978-1-4271-7791-9 (electronic html)
 1. English language--Synonyms and antonyms--Juvenile literature. 2.
English language--Parts of speech--Juvenile literature. 3. English language--
Grammar--Juvenile literature. 4. Language arts (Primary) 5. Language arts
(Elementary) I. Title. II. Title: Book of synonyms and antonyms.

 PE1591.J66 2015
 428'.1--dc23
                                                       2014045070

Crabtree Publishing Company

www.crabtreebooks.com   1-800-387-7650

Printed in Canada/022015/IH20141209q

Published in Canada
Crabtree Publishing
616 Welland Ave.
St. Catharines, Ontario
L2M 5V6

Published in the United States
Crabtree Publishing
PMB 59051
350 Fifth Avenue, 59th Floor
New York, New York 10118

Published in the United Kingdom
Crabtree Publishing
Maritime House
Basin Road North, Hove
BN41 1WR

Published in Australia
Crabtree Publishing
3 Charles Street
Coburg North
VIC 3058

Contents

Magic words

Words are magical things! They give you wings to fly. They let you soar high and low. Words help you catch giant dragons. They let you rescue little princes. Words make you jump for joy. You bounce up and down on the bed. Then you crawl under the covers for a bedtime story.

Synonyms and antonyms

There are all kinds of magic words! Some words are **synonyms**. Synonyms mean the same thing as other words. Some words are **antonyms**. Antonyms have opposite meanings to other words. We use words to share our ideas. We also use them to ask and answer questions. The Word Wizards use words to make magic! They need your help to learn some new magic words.

Words give you wings!

5

Synonyms are words that mean the same thing or nearly the same thing as other words. The words "tasty," "yummy," and "delicious" are synonyms. They all describe something that tastes good. They have the same **definition**. A definition is the meaning of a word.

This girl sees something good to eat!

Adjectives and verbs

Some synonyms are **adjectives**. Adjectives describe words called **nouns**. Nouns name people, animals, places, things, or ideas. The synonyms "happy" and "glad" are adjectives. We can use them to describe people.

Some synonyms are **verbs**. Verbs are action words. They tell what people or things are doing. The synonyms "smile" and "grin" are verbs. They describe what happy people do.

This girl has a huge sandwich and a big grin!

How do you think this boy feels? Use synonyms to describe him.

How are synonyms helpful?

Synonyms help us tell stories. They let us use different words. Different words make our stories interesting. Without synonyms, books would be boring! We would fall asleep reading them. We would snooze. We would nap. We would doze. We would snore.

This boy fell asleep while reading. His book did not have any synonyms.

Word Wizard
in training

Synonyms let you choose different words. The more words you know, the more choices you have. Look at the word web below. It shows synonyms for the word "pretty." Can you help the Word Wizard read them? Some of the synonyms are pretty big! But you are pretty smart. You are pretty clever. You can do it!

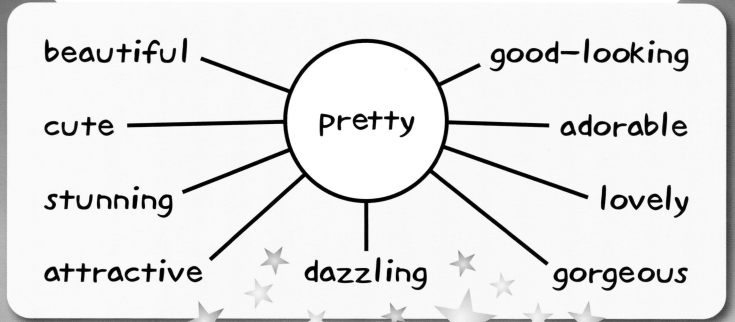

beautiful

cute

stunning

attractive

pretty

dazzling

good-looking

adorable

lovely

gorgeous

Almost the same

Some words have **similar** meanings. Similar means they are alike. They are not exactly the same, though. There are small differences in their meanings. The adjectives "chilly" and "freezing" both mean "cold." The word "chilly" means it is cool. The word "freezing" means it is really cold. You better bundle up!

This boy looks really cool!

It is freezing cold outside. Even the snowman needs a scarf!

Shades of meaning

Small differences in words are called **shades of meaning**. Some words have weaker meanings. They have less power or force than other words. Other words have stronger meanings. They are more powerful words. We can choose weak or strong words to tell our stories.

strong

hurl
fling
pitch
throw
toss

weak

This girl is ready for the beach! Will she toss, throw, or hurl the ball? Will she build a tall or towering sandcastle?

What do you mean?

Shades of meaning let you say exactly what you mean. They let you choose the best words for your stories. They help you paint pictures with words. These girls painted pictures with brushes! Use colorful words to describe them.

Word Wizard
in training

Help the Word Wizard finish these **sentences**. Sentences are complete thoughts or ideas. Point to a word to fill in each blank. Choose words you think tell the story best. Look at the pictures for clues.

This girl baked some cookies. Now the kitchen is _____! dusty dirty filthy

This wizard made some cookies, too! He _____ his magic wand to make them. moved waved shook

A thesaurus is not a dinosaur!

Have you ever seen a **thesaurus**? It sounds like a dinosaur, but it is not! A thesaurus is a book. It lists words and their synonyms. It helps you choose words for your stories. You can find thesauruses at the library. You can also find them on computers.

This boy needs a synonym for his story. A thesaurus will help him!

*A **dictionary** is a book, too. It gives you definitions of words.*

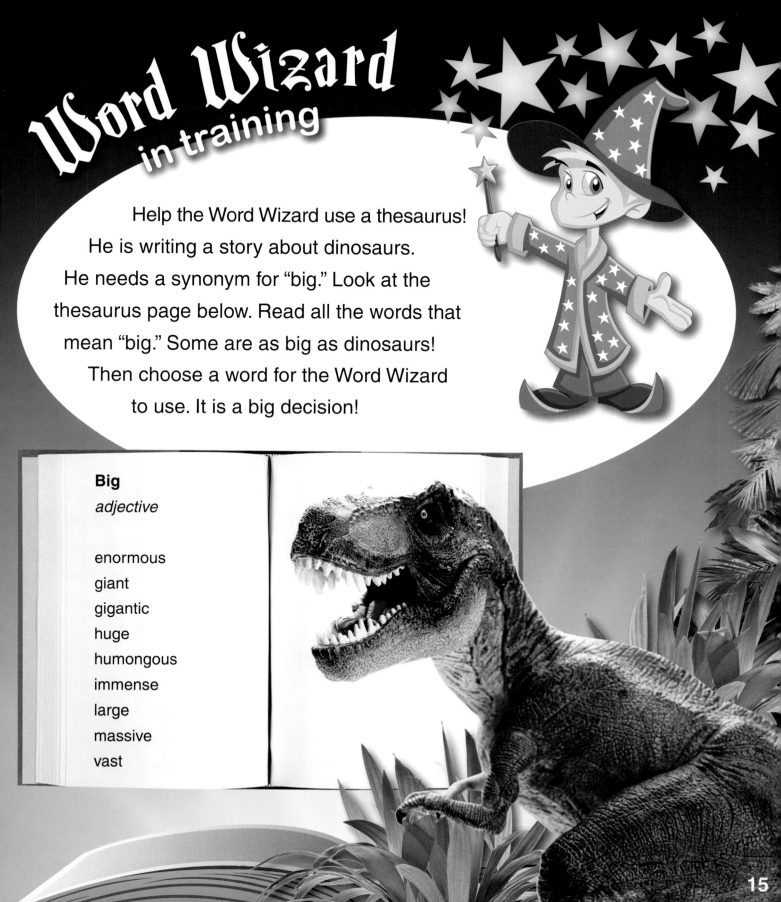

Word Wizard in training

Help the Word Wizard use a thesaurus! He is writing a story about dinosaurs. He needs a synonym for "big." Look at the thesaurus page below. Read all the words that mean "big." Some are as big as dinosaurs! Then choose a word for the Word Wizard to use. It is a big decision!

Big

adjective

enormous
giant
gigantic
huge
humongous
immense
large
massive
vast

Antonyms are opposites

Most thesauruses also list antonyms. Antonyms are two words that mean the **opposite** or nearly the opposite of each other. Opposite means completely different. The adjectives "good" and "bad" are antonyms. The verbs "push" and "pull" are antonyms, too.

Are these girls pushing or pulling the toy? Are they being good or bad?

Word Wizard in training

Help the Word Wizard match the antonyms below. Use your finger to join the words. Are they adjectives or verbs? Remember that adjectives tell us more about things. Verbs are action words.

old	white
give	sell
black	young
sit	cold
hot	stand
buy	take

Lemonade

How are antonyms helpful?

Antonyms let us **contrast** words. Contrast means to **compare** two things to show how they are different. We stop at red lights. We go at green lights. "Stop" is the antonym of "go." A car is fast. A turtle is slow. "Fast" is the antonym of "slow." Antonyms help us tell how things are different.

These kids are waiting for a green light. Then they can cross the street safely.

A turtle is slow when it walks. It is fast when it rides a skateboard!

Word Wizard in training

Help the Word Wizard finish these sentences. Tell him antonyms that could fill in the blanks. Choose words that contrast the red words. Look at the pictures for clues.

One boy looks happy, but the other looks _____.

One dog is huge, but the other is _____.

Different and the same

Synonyms and antonyms are different. Synonyms give you word choices. Antonyms let you contrast words. Synonyms and antonyms are also the same in some ways. They both make your **vocabulary** bigger. Your vocabulary is all the words you know. Now you can add the word "vocabulary" to your vocabulary!

Synonyms and antonyms help your vocabulary grow!

Show and tell

Synonyms and antonyms also help you **communicate**. To communicate means to share ideas and information. We communicate in many ways. We ask and answer questions in class. We show our toys. We tell our stories. How else do we communicate?

This girl is pleased with her picture. She is proud to show it to the class.

This boy uses sign language to communicate. He is signing the antonyms "up" and "down."

Sometimes we whisper when we communicate. Other times we scream!

Make word magic

Now it is time to make your own thesaurus! Get some paper, a pencil, and some markers. Use the pencil to write down an adjective. "Good" and "small" are adjectives you could use. Or think of your own. Now choose a verb. The words "walk" and "talk" are verbs. What other verbs do you know?

Add synonyms and antonyms

Write down some synonyms for each word. Then list some antonyms. Use the markers to add pictures if you like. You can use your thesaurus to write a story. You can make magic with words. You can be a Word Wizard!

These big kids are telling a giant story!

Learning more

Books

If You Were an Antonym (Word Fun) by Nancy Loewen. Picture Window Books, 2007.

If You Were a Synonym (Word Fun) by Michael Dahl. Picture Window Books, 2007.

Scholastic Children's Thesaurus by John K. Bollard. Scholastic Inc., 2006.

Slap Shot Synonyms and Antonyms (Grammar All-Stars) by Anna Prokos. Gareth Stevens Publishing, 2009.

Straight and Curvy, Meek and Nervy: More about Antonyms (Words Are CATegorical) by Brian P. Cleary. Millbrook Press, 2014.

Stroll and Walk, Babble and Talk: More about Synonyms (Words Are CATegorical) by Brian P. Cleary. Millbrook Press, 2014.

Websites

Help Synonym Sam and her dog find synonyms in this fun PBS Kids game.
http://pbskids.org/lions/games/synsam.html

Visit this website to play an antonym matching game with the Opposite Bunny.
http://pbskids.org/lions/games/hopposites.html

Toss balls and hit synonyms and antonyms in this super game.
www.abcya.com/synonyms_antonyms.htm

Turn and match synonym cards in this memory game from PBS Kids.
http://pbskids.org/superwhy/#/game/superwhyconcentration

Words to know

adjective (AJ-ik-tiv) A word that describes a person, animal, place, thing, or idea

antonym (AN-tuh-nim) A word that means the opposite or nearly the opposite of another word

communicate (kuh-MYOO-ni-keyt) To share ideas and information

compare (kuhm-PAIR) To tell what is the same or different

contrast (KON-trast) To compare two things to show how they are different

definition (def-uh-NISH-uh n) The meaning of a word

dictionary (DIK-shuh-ner-ee) A book that gives the meanings of words

noun (noun) A word that names a person, animal, place, thing, or idea

opposite (OP-uh-sit) Totally different

sentence (SEN-tns) A complete thought or idea

shades of meaning (sheyds uhv MEE-ning) Small differences in the meaning of words

similar (SIM-uh-ler) Almost the same as someone or something else

synonym (SIN-uh-nim) A word that means the same thing or nearly the same thing as another word

thesaurus (thi-SAWR-uh s) A book that gives synonyms and antonyms for words

verb (vurb) A word that tells what a person or thing is doing

vocabulary (voh-KAB-yuh-ler-ee) All the words a person knows and uses

Index